campaigns. If these concepts c  will work anywhere!"

—Bob Beckel, political st
   *Common Ground*

"The best time to have learned this secret is many years ago; the second best time is NOW. I'm so, so very glad I read this book!"

—Bob Burg, coauthor of *The Go-Giver*

"I cannot begin to tell you how many times I quote *The 4th Secret of the One Minute Manager* and all I have learned from it. It really has affected my management style and the corporate approach at Colin Cowie Lifestyle. I have watched so many of my employees blossom and grow because of it."

—Colin Cowie, author, television personality and celebrated designer

"The real value of *The 4th Secret* is what comes next: Without taking responsibility, you can't fix the problem, and you probably won't learn anything."

—Robert Engler, M.D., professor of medicine emeritus, cardiovascular research consultant

"Whether you're an entrepreneur or corporate executive, *The 4th Secret* is a MUST READ! I'd call this one of the MOST important secrets to succeeding in business."

—Cameron Johnson, author of *You Call the Shots*

"I will use this sage, practical advice, and hope everyone else will do the same. Teach this method to your loved ones, friends and everyone else whose lives you touch."
—George Pratt, Ph.D., chairman, psychology, Scripps Memorial Hospital, La Jolla, California, and coauthor of *Instant Emotional Healing*

"Thank you, Margret McBride and Ken Blanchard, for turning on a lot of lightbulbs!"
—Lynn Schenk, California congresswoman (fmr.)

"There are few things as liberating as the willingness to freely admit a mistake. And what could be simpler? Blanchard and McBride have provided us with how to say those three little words that mean so much: 'I was wrong.' Everyone could benefit from *The Fourth Secret!*"
—Susan Polis Schutz, cofounder of Blue Mountain Arts, author of *To My Daughter With Love on the Important Things in Life*

"We are all managers: managers of others, managers of ourselves—professionally and personally. *The 4th Secret of the One Minute Manager* guides the reader through an easily applicable process that results in honesty and integrity for the everyday manager."
—Gayle Tauber, cofounder of Kashi Cereal Company

"This is a very important and elegant parable. With the realistic admission to ourselves and to others that we have made a mistake, humanity becomes wiser."
—Marshall Thurber, founder of the Positive Deviant Network

"I have never met anyone who didn't have moments where an apology wasn't in order. Not just any apology will do, however. *The 4th Secret* gives clear and compelling insights into the wrong way and correct way to apologize. It is an amazing and simple rebound strategy when our words or actions have brought harm to others."
—Mick Ukleja, founder of the Ukleja Center for Ethical Leadership, California State University, Long Beach; and coauthor of *Who Are You and What Do You Want?*

"The most compelling thing about this book is the emphasis it puts not only on the importance of honestly confronting a mistake but taking responsibility and changing behavior—not just words but the actions."
—Mary Lindenstein Walshok, associate vice chancellor, University of California, San Diego

"As a teacher for the San Diego County juvenile court and community schools, I have daily contact with children and parents unable to effectively communicate with each other. Families will benefit from reading this book together: They will learn a powerful method for maintaining emotionally healthy relationships."

—Trudy Atchison, M.A. Ed.

"*The 4th Secret* offers timeless lessons on facing reality. This simple advice is priceless."

—Rosanne Badowski, executive assistant to Jack Welch and author of *Managing Up*

"It's a must-read. Any person in any type of relationship —marital, filial, or professional—has to read this book. The story of Lincoln's apology will be an example to me for the rest of my life."

—Joel Bauer, vice chairman, Department of Surgery, Mount Sinai School of Medicine, New York

"*The 4th Secret of the One Minute Manager* is a book that can change your life. It can even change the world. Buy it. Read it. Make it part of your life. You won't be sorry!"

—Sheldon Bowles, coauthor of *Gung Ho!* and *Raving Fans*

"A quick, enjoyable read that has the power to accomplish a lasting and profound personal transformation. It's a message that will resonate from the boardroom to the mailroom."

—Roger Gittines, coauthor of *Managing Up* and *Don't Fire Them, Fire Them Up!*

"The book you need to help repair business or personal relationships that otherwise might be lost."

> —Paula Hauer, former vice president, Dow Theory Letters, Inc.

"In *The 4th Secret* Ken Blanchard and Margret McBride give you not just the whys and the hows, but the actual words to use."

> —Marjorie Hansen Shaevitz, M.A., M.F.C.C., author of *The Superwoman Syndrome* and *The Confident Woman*

"The beauty of *The 4th Secret* is its simplicity. It's the golden rule expanded to fit every situation, and anyone can use it in their workplace or just to make their lives better."

> —Jeanne Jones, author of the syndicated column "Cook It Light"

"*The 4th Secret of the One Minute Manager* is an ode to humility. In concise, simple language it carries a profound message: that leaders must not be afraid to admit their mistakes and correct them instantly."

> —Laurence Kirshbaum, founder and president, LJK Literary Management

"Ken Blanchard and Margret McBride have created a simple yet powerful little book that helps us all bridge the gap between the 'shoulda dones' and the 'dids' of

day-to-day life. A quantum leap into compassion. You'll feel better for it."
—Kenny Loggins, singer, composer and author

"One of the most important success factors is the willingness to admit you were wrong. *The 4th Secret of the One Minute Manager* is a must-read."
—Paul J. Meyer, founder of Success Motivation, Inc., coauthor of *Chicken Soup for the Golden Soul* and author of *Unlocking Your Legacy*

"A business parable for our time that reminds us all of the values of integrity, honesty and self-respect. An invaluable resource for anyone who needs to say they're sorry."
—Robert J. Nugent, former chairman and CEO, Jack in the Box, Inc.

"McBride and Blanchard offer readers a simple yet effective way to understand and implement emotional healing in the aftermath of life's missteps."
—Stephen M. Pfeiffer, Ph.D., executive director of the Association for the Advancement of Psychology

"This marvelous book makes a compelling case for having one of the fiercest conversations known to man. This book shows us how."
—Susan Scott, author of *Fierce Conversations*

"Every businessperson needs to read this book. I am ordering copies for everyone I work and do business with. Most businesspeople do not realize how empowering a One Minute Apology can be in their professional and personal interactions."

—Ivor Royston, M.D., managing member of Forward Ventures, San Diego, California

*"The 4th Secret of the One Minute Manager* is an instant classic and worthy companion to *The One Minute Manager.* It's must-reading and especially timely in the post-Enron business world."

—Sheldon Siegel, San Francisco attorney and bestselling author

"Our work and our world cannot do without the messages in *The 4th Secret.* Read this remarkable, beautiful and essential book. Get back to where you once belonged."

—Stan Slap, international management consultant

# The 4th Secret of the One Minute Manager®

# Also by Ken Blanchard

LEADING AT A HIGHER LEVEL (with the Founding Associates and Consulting Partners of the Ken Blanchard Companies), 2006

SELF LEADERSHIP AND THE ONE MINUTE MANAGER (with Susan Fowler and Laurence Hawkins), 2005

THE LEADERSHIP PILL (with Marc Muchnick), 2003

FULL STEAM AHEAD (with Jesse Stoner), 2003

THE SERVANT LEADER (with Phil Hodges), 2003

THE ONE MINUTE APOLOGY (with Margret McBride), 2003

ZAP THE GAPS! (with Dana Robinson and Jim Robinson), 2002

WHALE DONE! (with Thad Lacinak, Chuck Tompkins, and Jim Ballard), 2002

HIGH FIVE! (with Sheldon Bowles), 2000

MANAGEMENT OF ORGANIZATIONAL BEHAVIOR: UTILIZING HUMAN RESOURCES (with Paul Hersey), 8th edition, 2000

BIG BUCKS! (with Sheldon Bowles), 2000

LEADERSHIP BY THE BOOK (with Bill Hybels and Phil Hodges), 1999

THE HEART OF A LEADER, 1999

GUNG HO! (with Sheldon Bowles), 1998

MANAGEMENT BY VALUES (with Michael O'Connor), 1997

MISSION POSSIBLE (with Terry Waghorn), 1996

EMPOWERMENT TAKES MORE THAN A MINUTE (with John P. Carlos and Alan Randolph), 1996

EVERYONE'S A COACH (with Don Shula), 1995

RAVING FANS (with Sheldon Bowles), 1993

PLAYING THE GREAT GAME OF GOLF, 1992

THE ONE MINUTE MANAGER BUILDS HIGH PERFORMING TEAMS (with Don Carew and Eunice Parisi-Carew), 1990

THE ONE MINUTE MANAGER MEETS THE MONKEY (with William Oncken, Jr., and Hal Burrows), 1989

THE POWER OF ETHICAL MANAGEMENT (with Norman Vincent Peale), 1988

THE ONE MINUTE MANAGER GETS FIT (with D. W. Edington and Marjorie Blanchard), 1986

LEADERSHIP AND THE ONE MINUTE MANAGER (with Patricia Zigarmi and Drea Zigarmi), 1985

ORGANIZATIONAL CHANGE THROUGH EFFECTIVE LEADERSHIP (with Robert H. Guest and Paul Hersey), 2nd edition, 1985

PUTTING THE ONE MINUTE MANAGER TO WORK (with Robert Lorber), 1984

THE ONE MINUTE MANAGER (with Spencer Johnson), 1982

# The 4th Secret of the One Minute Manager®

## A Powerful Way to Make Things Better

Previously published under the title *The One Minute Apology*

## Ken Blanchard and Margret McBride

*WM*

**WILLIAM MORROW**
*An Imprint of* HarperCollins*Publishers*

Grateful acknowledgment is made for permission to reprint the following: Excerpt from chapter 23, "The Draft-Decision-Pathos" in *Abraham Lincoln: The War Years*, volume III, Sangamon Edition by Carl Sandburg, copyright 1939 by Harcourt, Inc., and renewed 1967 by Carl Sandburg, reprinted by permission of Harcourt, Inc.

HarperCollins books may be purchased for educational, business, or sales promotional use. For information please write: Special Markets Department, HarperCollins Publishers, 10 East 53rd Street, New York, NY 10022.

FIRST EDITION

*Designed by Nancy Singer Olaguera*

Library of Congress Cataloging-in-Publication Data
has been applied for.

ISBN 978-0-06-147031-8

08   09   10   11   12   ID/RRD   10   9   8   7   6   5   4   3   2   1

*To all of us who could have made life better at work and at home with a few well-timed and sincerely delivered apologies.*

# Contents

Foreword by Spencer Johnson, M.D.   ix
The Journey   1
The Fourth Secret   8
Honesty   23
Integrity   33
Not Attached To Outcome   55
Apology At Home and Work   58
Taking Responsibility   73
Confidence   77
Apologizing To Yourself   83
Asking For a One Minute Apology   87
A Chance To Finally Get It Right   92
The Best Way To Say Thank You   95
The Moment Of Truth   100
The President's One Minute Apology   108
Epilogue   115
*Acknowledgments*   121
*Services Available*   123

# Foreword

Spencer Johnson, M.D.

*The 4th Secret of the One Minute Manager* is the story of a corporate leader who, in the middle of these changing times, has made the kind of mistake we see all too often in the headlines of our newspapers.

It is easy to wonder how such smart and apparently successful people can get so far off track and lose sight of what's really important. Then, all too often, we see them compound their mistake by not acknowledging that they are wrong and not apologizing for what they have done in a way that makes good sense—by changing their behavior.

And of course if we watch the real-life drama unfold, the situation, uncorrected, usually gets worse. Yet how many of us can see ourselves in these stories—even though we may not have similar positions or have made similar mistakes? We have all invariably made mistakes of our own.

In the story that follows, you can discover what you can do in business or life to recognize when you have been wrong and to apologize to the people you harmed in a way that can make a bad situation into a better one.

Few things are more powerful than having the common sense, wisdom, and strength to admit when you've made a mistake and to set things right.

Ken Blanchard and Margret McBride show us a great way to deal with our mistakes successfully through the eyes of a young man who learns the secrets of a meaningful apology.

In the opening chapter, we see the company president's dilemma. Then the young man goes to The One Minute Manager's summer lake home, where he gains important insights into how he can help.

The young man's journey brings us to our own discoveries about what we can do to make things better, at work or at home, with our own one minute apologies.

If our leaders used this book to make needed changes, our world would be a better place to live in. But why wait? We can use *The 4th Secret of the One Minute Manager* ourselves to improve our *own* world and enjoy the tremendous results.

*The 4th Secret of the One Minute Manager* is more than a technique. And it is certainly more than just words. It is a useful way to think and live more successfully.

I hope you enjoy reading the story and benefiting from it as much as I have.

## The Journey

Once there was a bright young man named Matt who set out on a life-changing journey. A major crisis at the company where he worked troubled him greatly and sent him on his quest. Little did he know that he would soon learn about a secret power that was known to only a few, but would soon be valued by many people throughout the world.

It was a Friday before a three-day Fourth of July holiday weekend. An emergency meeting of the board of directors was in progress in the company's boardroom. Matt's boss, the photogenic and dynamic president and CEO, David J. Roberts, was speaking from the head of a long table.

At first, Roberts spoke confidently as he described the nature of the company's problem. However, his demeanor changed when members of the board responded with specific questions:

*How long has this been going on? When was the first time you learned of this? Why didn't you take action before now? Couldn't you have seen what the consequences of such actions might be?*

Refusing to take responsibility, Roberts became angry and defensive, which only made things worse. His voice became louder, his tone harsher, and his attitude more stubborn.

The board members had never heard Roberts talk like this before. When he stopped, everyone in the room was silent, stunned by what had just happened.

As Roberts's chief assistant, Matt Hawkins had been in many other board meetings at the president's request, but he'd never seen one like this. The president's behavior came as a shock, because Matt so admired him. As a matter of fact, right after Matt graduated from business school, Roberts had recognized his potential and gave him his first big opportunity.

What would happen now?

*Is this the beginning of the end?* Matt thought, feeling his heart sink. *How will our company survive?*

He knew that David Roberts needed to take a new course of action, or everybody's position would be in jeopardy. Indeed, even the future of the company was at stake now.

Matt listened as the chairman of the board addressed the president.

"Well, we've heard all of your excuses and rationalizations," the chairman began. "Frankly, I am unimpressed. If we don't resolve this quickly, our company's reputation will be ruined, along with our stock value.

"On Tuesday morning after the holiday weekend," the chairman continued, "we will meet here again. Because of your history with us, you deserve an opportunity to set the record straight. Between now and then think carefully about what you plan to do and what you will say to us. If you haven't come up with an effective way to restore our confidence, we may have to look for new leadership."

The chairman abruptly called for adjournment. Visibly shaken, Roberts stood up to leave the room.

Matt rose from his chair and opened the boardroom door for his boss. As the president strode past, he signaled for Matt to follow him to his waiting car.

"Please leave word on my voice mail where you are going to be this weekend in case I need to reach you," Roberts said. "If possible, I would like you to join me in my office at 7:00 A.M. Monday to prepare for Tuesday's meeting."

As the car sped away, a sense of dread came over Matt. He knew his boss was making a huge mistake. Everyone on the board seemed to see it except the president himself. Matt thought, *What can I do to help?*

Back in his office, Matt pondered the situation. What could his president possibly say to the board of directors Tuesday morning to avoid his downfall? *Where can I find the answers that will help him see things differently and set things right?* Matt wondered.

Then he remembered his late father's advice: "If you ever need help, call my good friend, Jack Peterson. There's a good reason everyone refers to him as The One Minute Manager. He's the only person I've met who can simplify complicated issues in a way you will know exactly what to do—and then be able to do it in a minute. He's my most trusted friend and he'll always be there for you."

Matt called Jack Peterson's office and learned that Jack was vacationing at his lake house with his wife, Carol, and their kids, Annie and Brad. Hearing that brought back many happy memories of when he and his family visited them every summer. Brad and Annie were almost like a brother and a sister to him. Yet it had been five years since his last visit and now he regretted not staying in touch.

Matt left a message on Jack's voice mail summarizing the problem and saying that he needed expert advice by Monday at the latest, but certainly understood if Jack didn't want to interrupt his vacation with his family.

Later at his apartment, Matt got the call he was waiting for.

"Of course, I'd love to help you!" Jack said enthusiastically. "There's a powerful new secret I've been teaching people. It sounds like it's exactly what your president needs right now. Once people put this secret into practice, they solve problems and improve relationships in ways they never believed possible."

"I can't wait to hear all about it," said Matt.

"It's more than we can cover in this phone call. Join us for the weekend! You'll see your problem from a new perspective up here at the lake. Bring your golf clubs and we'll have fun as we solve your problem. Carol just booked you on the 7:30 P.M. commuter flight and Brad is picking you up at the airport. Annie arrives tomorrow morning. We're all excited about seeing you! Everyone here is an expert on the new secret—including Nana!"

Matt's spirits soared and he immediately accepted.

"Regarding my new secret," said Jack, "on your way here you might give this some thought:

�֍

*The Toughest Part*
*Of Turning Around*
*A Bad Situation*
*Is Realizing*
*And*
*Admitting*
*That*
*You Were Wrong*

�֍

## The Fourth Secret

On the way to the airport, Matt called the president's voice mail, told him where he could be reached and confirmed the Monday morning meeting. Hearing the president's voice mail greeting rekindled Matt's anxiety.

After Matt's flight landed, Brad met him at baggage claim. They gave each other a hearty hug and talked the entire drive to the lake house. When they arrived, Jack and his wife, Carol, greeted Matt warmly and told him how happy they were that he was back. As he walked through the living room, Matt noticed that little had changed. The cozy, comfortable furnishings still invited a wonderful sense of relaxation.

Jack offered Matt a cold drink and they all spent time catching up on one another's lives. Then Brad and Carol excused themselves to give Jack and Matt time to talk privately.

Jack got right to the point. "You are here for such a short time, let's set some goals about what you want to accomplish this weekend."

"My first One Minute Goal is to get your advice about how I might help my president. Under different circumstances, I would love to play golf with you, but getting a handle on this problem could take all weekend. If only things could have gone differently. Maybe I should have—"

"Matt, you'll have plenty of time to do anything you like and solve your problem," Jack replied, "once you stop using phrases like *should have, could have, would have* and *if only*. Those are 'worry words.' They make you feel overwhelmed, discouraged and confused. They are time wasters that keep you stuck in the past and prevent you from moving forward with your best course of action. They also get in the way of being honest with yourself."

Matt looked puzzled.

Jack smiled and said, "Do you want to look back on this weekend as a time spent agonizing over things from the past that you can't change? Or do you want to remember it as the weekend you learned a powerful new way to make things better?"

"Of course, I'd rather learn how to make things better," answered Matt.

"Then let's go outside. The fresh air has a great effect on me and I do my best thinking outside. That's why I like to come up here." He got up and led Matt to the porch overlooking the lake.

Matt looked out at the pine trees silhouetted against the hills, the moon reflecting on the water below, and the lights flickering from the cabins across the lake.

Jack sat in one of the deck chairs and motioned for Matt to do the same. "Before we get started, let me share something important with you."

"Of course."

"Do you know what appealed to me most about your voice mail?"

"What?"

"You said you worked for someone you had admired, the company was in trouble, and you wanted to find a way to help. Do you know how rare that is? Many people say, 'Hey, that's not my problem.' They separate themselves from the situation and steer clear of anyone involved. Mentally, they jump ship. Once things blow over, they act as if nothing happened. When someone as loyal as you cares enough to stay involved, I'll go to any length to help."

"Thanks, but don't forget that David Roberts gave me a wonderful opportunity after I graduated," Matt replied. "I learned a lot from him when he was at his best. He was a really great mentor. I wouldn't feel very good about myself if I bailed out on him and the company when I know both are in trouble."

"I admire your attitude."

"Thank you," said Matt. "I also enjoy being part of a dynamic company and believe it's still possible for us to have a bright future. I'd like to understand how things went so wrong, so fast. The whole situation is now such a mess. I hardly know where to begin."

The moon rose higher and shimmered on the lake as Matt described what happened. When he finished, Jack turned to him and said, "Given what you have just told me, I agree that this situation is more serious than I expected. I understand why you're concerned. If some well-thought-out action isn't taken soon, your whole company could go down—and very very quickly at that."

After a pause, Jack continued, "The fact is, there is only *one* thing your president can do to make things dramatically better for everyone concerned."

"In your phone call you spoke about a new secret. Is that what you have in mind?" asked Matt.

"Absolutely. Done properly, it's one of the most powerful things anyone can do to repair a bad situation —even one as serious as your president's."

"Please tell me all about it," replied Matt.

"For more than twenty-five years I have been using three management secrets," said Jack.

"I know," interjected Matt. "One Minute Goals, One Minute Praising and One Minute Reprimands. They're known as the One Minute Manager's three secrets. I use them all the time."

Jack smiled, saying, "Yes, I noticed when you mentioned your One Minute Goal for this weekend. You remember well. Over the years I've been asked to teach the three secrets to corporations, and now they're used in businesses and organizations of all kinds, including schools and hospitals around the world. People value the three secrets because they work. Recently, someone asked me, 'What happens when managers use the three secrets to set goals, decide who and when to praise and reprimand, but they get it wrong? All managers make mistakes once in a while. When they're wrong, how can they get back on track—fast and effectively?'

"That's when I knew it was time to introduce the fourth secret—The One Minute Apology. This secret boils down to a One Minute point: *the minute you realize you have made a mistake, you need to apologize.*"

Matt said, "That makes sense, but in this situation my president has made some very serious mistakes. Will apologizing be enough?"

"Not if the apology is empty words," Jack said. "The power of the One Minute Apology lies with a person's actions, intentions and sincerity, not in what they say."

"Because what they say may have no real meaning," added Matt.

Jack nodded.

Matt opened his journal and wrote:

*The Power of*
*The One Minute Apology*
*Is More Than*
*Just Words*

"You call it the One Minute Apology, which makes it sound simple, yet I get the sense there's a lot more to apologizing than I used to think," observed Matt.

"Dishonesty poisons relationships and the consequences are dire," Jack said. "For example, if your president doesn't admit his mistakes and deal with them right away, he'll lose the trust and respect of the board, and careers and relationships will be damaged."

"So apologizing has the potential not only to correct a wrong, but also to restore the confidence others have had in you. What should he do first?"

"He needs to make an obvious change in his behavior. For a start, he can drop his arrogant attitude and get back to being human again. With a One Minute Apology he can step up to the plate, admit he was wrong and deal with what really caused the damage—instead of distracting everyone with the symptoms."

"It's hard to believe my president could do all of that in a minute," remarked Matt.

"That's why it's called the One Minute Apology—it can be said in a minute once you know how to do it. Thinking it through is the part that takes time. What most people forget is that no one wants to listen to an apology for more than a minute!

"In a One Minute Apology, there is no time for excuses, self-victimization or drama. It's simple, to-the-point, clear and very effective. *Saying it takes only a minute but becoming completely honest with yourself and taking responsibility for your mistakes before you apologize takes longer.* Unless you do that, it won't be effective."

"I see," said Matt thoughtfully.

"Your president's problem," said Jack, "as with that of many leaders in similar situations today, began when he was unwilling to admit to himself that he did something wrong. It's his job to accept responsibility for his actions. In your president's case, he's captain of a ship that's going under fast. But he isn't the only one going down; he's taking the company—everyone's livelihood and future—with him, rather than confronting his problems.

"As you get older, Matt, you'll discover that the core of most problems is the same," said Jack. "Only the names, dates and places change."

"What's the core of most problems?" Matt asked.

✸

*At The Core*
*Of*
*Most Problems*
*Is*
*A Truth*
*That Is Being Denied*

✸

Jack continued, "*Any problem begins to spin out of control the minute you avoid dealing with the truth.*"

"I think you've identified my president's problem," Matt said. "When I first met Roberts, I thought he was a champion among champions, a model of integrity—someone who wanted to hear and speak the truth. But as his success increased, he began to lose touch with reality. His growing sense of self-importance has made it difficult for him to admit the truth and do the right thing. I'm even concerned that he has lost sight of what the right thing is anymore."

"People who pretend 'it never happened' or that 'it wasn't my fault' are in denial because they've lost touch with the truth. They can't apologize because they rationalize that they're not at fault. They can't admit they are wrong."

"Why don't people want to face the truth?" wondered Matt.

"They're afraid to confront the truth," began Jack. "There is either right or wrong. The truth of right or wrong doesn't give people much 'wiggle room,' and for some, that feels very uncomfortable—especially if they're living a lie. They don't know how freeing the truth is, because they've never really experienced it."

Matt immediately caught on. "That explains why my president is defensive and unwilling to listen to criticism. Lately if anyone tries to tell him the truth, he shoots the messenger. I've found myself keeping anyone or anything with negative information from my boss, just to prevent him from getting angry and taking it out on me and the other members of the staff. The serious implications of what you're saying are getting to me. I have a lot to think about right now. I'd like to take some time to let this sink in."

"That's a good idea," said Jack. "Why don't we call it a day?"

"I agree. So, I guess we've pretty much covered the subject of the One Minute Apology?" Matt asked, rubbing his tired eyes.

"No, we've only touched the surface. There are two vital parts of the One Minute Apology that we'll cover tomorrow: honesty and integrity. As you'll see:

✻

*A One Minute Apology*
*Begins With*
*Honesty*
*And*
*Ends With*
*Integrity*

✻

"Annie arrives in the morning. Why don't you talk with her about the first part of the One Minute Apology—*honesty*. She knows the topic inside and out. Then, after breakfast, we'll motor across the lake to see someone who's looking forward to seeing you—my mother, Nana. We're going to join her to pick vegetables from her garden for tomorrow's 4th of July dinner. We hope you'll join us. Nana has great advice about the second part of the One Minute Apology—*integrity*. Later in the afternoon we can play golf, if you like."

"I really think I should be concentrating on having a plan for my meeting with Roberts on Monday morning," said Matt.

Jack chuckled. "Life is not all work, Matt—it's also about having some fun, too. Being able to take time to do something you enjoy while you're solving problems is a sign that you are in charge of your life."

"My father said I could always trust you to steer me in the right direction," Matt said, walking toward his room. "Dad, as usual, was right! See you in the morning."

"Your dad was my best friend and I sure miss him. It's like old times having you here with us. Glad you came up. Good night, Matthew."

# *Honesty*

Saturday morning, Matt awoke at seven o'clock, went to the kitchen, and made a pot of coffee. He took his notebook and coffee outside, careful not to disturb anyone. When he got to the end of the dock, he sat down and watched the neighbors on their docks, decorating their boats, putting up flags and stringing lights in preparation for the 4th of July celebration that evening.

Reviewing his notes from the previous night, Matt was soon engrossed about ways he might apply what he was learning to his problem at work. Soon he was interrupted by the sound of tires on the driveway. He looked up to see Jack, Carol and Brad come out to greet the driver of the car. He knew from their enthusiastic expressions that it had to be Annie. Matt leapt up from his place on the dock and ran up the stairs two at a time.

"Dad said you were going to be here," Annie said as she gave him a warm hug. "It's great to see you."

Matt said, "Great to be here! It's been way too long, and I take full responsibility for that. Here, let me take your bag in."

"Who's hungry?" asked Carol.

"We are!" was the general consensus.

Over breakfast Annie asked, "I'm curious, Matt. What brought you back?"

"I have a problem at work and I'm looking for an answer. Your dad has been teaching me about the One Minute Apology."

Jack turned to his daughter and asked, "Annie, are you comfortable talking about—*honesty* and *admitting you were wrong*?"

"Considering all the practice I've had, I'd love to!" she joked, and everyone laughed as they recalled some of Annie's outrageous teenage escapades.

When the kidding subsided, Annie got serious, saying, "Honesty and admitting you are wrong are about *you* and coming to grips with what *you* did—and then making sure that anyone you harmed knows that *you* know you made a mistake. This requires being honest with yourself and letting go of being right. The way I think about it is:

❋

*One Minute*
*Of Being Honest*
*With Yourself*
*Is Worth More Than*
*Days, Months, Or Years*
*Of*
*Self-Deception*

❋

"Kidding yourself is an expensive habit that has no reward," said Annie.

"Self-deception comes at a high price," Matt agreed.

"Once you're honest with yourself," Annie continued, "take full responsibility for what you did and any harm done to someone else. That requires both humility *and* courage. Dad says great leaders give everyone else credit when things go well and take full responsibility when things go wrong. Whereas self-centered leaders take credit when things go well and blame everyone else when things go wrong."

Matt thought, *the self-centered leader describes my president's behavior in front of the board yesterday.*

"When you're honest, you let go of the contrived story or excuses you've told yourself and realize you need to apologize to anyone you've offended, regardless of the outcome," Annie said.

"How do you know when the person you've harmed understands that you now realize you made a mistake?" asked Matt.

"The most effective way is to first feel it yourself. That happens if you're honest with yourself, take action and admit to the other person that you were wrong. Think of it like this:

✲

*The Longer You Wait
To Apologize,
The Sooner
Your Mistake Is
Regarded As
A Weakness*

✲

"We all make mistakes. What loses the trust and respect of others is when we refuse to admit our mistakes. Then people conclude that if we can't be honest about this situation, we lie about other things, too."

"If that's the case, why don't people apologize sooner?" asked Matt.

Annie answered, "To some, apologizing is regarded as a weakness rather than a strength."

"Why?" Matt asked.

"Some people have a need to always be right," replied Annie.

"The problem with attempting to be right all the time is that you try to make someone else wrong," said Brad.

"Exactly," said Annie. "What an exhausting way to live—trying to be right all the time. If apologies were accepted as legitimate responses to making mistakes, then honesty would replace cover-ups. Anyone harmed could feel better right away."

"So," said Matt, "apologizing isn't just about ourselves, it's about the people we've wronged."

"Right. That's why it's important to be *specific*," said Annie, "and *say exactly what you're apologizing for.*"

Brad laughed. "When Annie and I were young, we were experts at vague apologies. If Mom or Dad caught us misbehaving, we'd say 'I'm sorry, I'm sorry, I'm sorry' until we were blue in the face."

"Did it work?" Matt asked.

"They *thought* it did," chuckled Carol.

Everyone laughed and Annie continued, "When you're specific about what you did wrong, share how you feel about what you did and admit that you're embarrassed, sad, or ashamed, you make your apology real."

"Without sharing your feelings," said Jack, "an apology will seem insincere and mechanical, like you're going through the motions without being personally involved. An apology has to feel authentic."

Matt admitted, "Maybe it's a guy thing, but describing *feelings* is one of the hardest things for me to do, especially in a situation where I'm already feeling bad or embarrassed."

"Don't ever think that women have the feelings subject cornered. It's easy to talk about feelings, but *expressing* your feelings to someone else is never easy. No one finds it easy to admit they are wrong," said Annie. "That's what I meant when I said apologizing takes both courage *and* humility."

Noticing everybody had finished eating, Matt said, "You've certainly given me a lot to chew on. Let me summarize what I've learned so far about how honesty makes a One Minute Apology work:

# A One Minute Apology Begins With Honesty

## You're Honest When You:

- *Admit to yourself that you've made a mistake and need to apologize.*

- *Have a sense of urgency and apologize as soon as possible.*

- *Tell anyone you've harmed specifically what you did wrong.*

- *Share any feelings or embarrassment you have about the mistake you made.*

# Integrity

After breakfast, Carol settled in on the living room couch to finish reading her book. Everyone else headed to the boat to motor across the lake to Nana's house.

They tied the boat to her dock and walked up a stone path. On each side was a flourishing vegetable garden filled with corn, zucchini, string beans, carrots, tomatoes, cucumbers, a variety of lettuces and eggplant.

Wearing a wide-brimmed gardening hat, overalls and canvas gloves, Nana greeted them. "Welcome! Why Matt, you look exactly like your father did when he was your age. Boy, did he and Jack have good times. It's sure great to have you back."

Matt gave her a big hug. "Nana, as soon as I learn to apologize properly, you'll be the first on my list. It's unforgivable I've stayed away five years."

"Almost six, but who's counting? I'm so happy you're here with us now," Nana said. "I've missed you."

"Thanks, Nana, I'm glad to be back," replied Matt. "I've never forgotten your amazing garden."

"All I do is plant the seeds. Nature is very forgiving of the mistakes I make," Nana said.

"We've just been talking about making mistakes," Matt said, "and the need to apologize for them."

"You're learning the One Minute Apology."

"Indeed I am," said Matt. "So far, I've learned about *honesty* from Annie. I hear I'm about to learn about the *integrity* part of a One Minute Apology. Jack says you have a lot of wisdom on the subject."

Nana smiled and said, "That's kind of you. Like my husband used to say, 'When all is said and done, the most important thing we have is our integrity.'"

"Is there a difference between honesty and integrity?" asked Matt.

"Yes," said Nana, adding:

✴

*Honesty*

*Is*

*Telling The Truth*

*To Ourselves And Others*

✴

*Integrity*

*Is*

*Living That Truth*

✴

"Admitting you made a mistake means you're honest," Matt reasoned, "and when you do what you say you're going to do—or as Jack calls it, 'walking your talk'—you have integrity."

"Good points," agreed Nana. "When you have integrity, you're honest regardless of the situation, who you're with, or where you are. It's up to each individual to become the person he or she wants to be."

"This may sound like a stupid question, but how do you determine the kind of person you want to be?" asked Matt.

"I'll tell you what I did. About ten years ago, I wrote my own obituary," said Jack with a smile.

"That sounds kind of morbid," said Matt.

Jack chuckled, saying, "I became interested in writing my own obituary after I heard a story about Alfred Nobel."

"Of the Nobel Peace Prize fame?"

"Yes," said Jack. "It's interesting. Even though the Nobel Prize is also given for Science, Economics, Literature, Medicine and Chemistry, Nobel is best known for the Peace Prize. Yet he wasn't always involved with peace. You might recall from history that Alfred Nobel was also involved with the invention of dynamite."

"Yes, now that you mention it," said Matt.

"After his brother died," continued Jack, "Alfred was reading the local Stockholm newspaper and had the unique experience of reading his own obituary. The paper had somehow mixed up the two brothers. Can you imagine what that must have felt like?"

"Did it describe his involvement with dynamite?" asked Matt.

"It did," said Jack. "So much so that Nobel was devastated to think that he would be remembered only for destruction. As a result, he redesigned his life so he would be remembered for honoring the pursuit of world peace. It became his driving motivation. How you want others to think about you in the future can determine the kind of person you want to be."

"So tell me if I have this right," said Matt. "Besides attempting to right a wrong, a One Minute Apology to yourself about your past is a way to realign who you have been with who you want to be?"

"That's a great way to think about it," said Jack. "One of my favorite sayings is:

✳

*The Legacy*
*You Leave*
*Is*
*The One*
*You Live*

✳

"No one's perfect," said Nana. "We all do things that are inconsistent with who we think we are. People measure your integrity by how quickly you correct your mistakes and get back on course."

"When you make amends to someone you've harmed, you feel better about yourself," said Matt.

"Absolutely," said Nana. "Continually remind yourself of your worth and good intentions by saying, 'I'm fine; it's my behavior that trips me up once in a while.' Never get upset with yourself—only with your behavior."

"That hits home with me. When my behavior is, shall we say, poorer than I want it to be, I keep thinking about what I did wrong and can't sleep at night. That is, until I correct my mistake," observed Matt.

"Like Abraham Lincoln," added Nana.

"Abraham Lincoln?" responded Matt.

"He's one of my heroes," said Nana. "Carl Sandburg wrote about Abe Lincoln's lapse in behavior and I reread it from time to time to help me remember that *everyone* makes mistakes. Let's take a break from the gardening and I'll show you that story."

Nana started up the stone steps toward her cottage, motioning for Matt to follow. She told Matt to have a seat on the porch while she looked for the book. When Nana returned, she opened the book and handed it to Matt. "This story shows how the challenges of leadership can test who you truly want to be."

Matt began to read:

During the Civil War President Abraham Lincoln was visited by Colonel Scott, one of the commanders of the troops guarding the Capitol from attack by the Confederate forces in Northern Virginia.

Scott's wife had drowned in a steamship collision in the Chesapeake Bay when returning home after a journey to Washington to nurse her sick husband.

Scott had appealed to regimental command for leave to attend her burial and comfort his children. His request had been denied; a battle seemed imminent and every officer was essential.

But Scott, as was his right, had pressed his request up the chain of command until it reached the Secretary of War, Edwin Stanton. Since Stanton had also denied the request, the colonel had taken his appeal all the way to the top.

Scott got to his Commander in Chief in the presidential office late on a Saturday night, the last visitor allowed in. Lincoln listened to the story and as Scott recalled his response, the President exploded, "Am I to have no rest? Is there no hour or spot when or where I may escape these constant requests? Why do you follow me here with such business as this? Why do you not go to the War Office where they have charge of all matters of papers and transportation?"

Scott told Lincoln of Stanton's refusal, and the President replied, "Then you probably ought not to go down the river. Mr. Stanton knows all about the necessities of the hour; he knows what rules are necessary, and the rules are made to be enforced.

"It would be wrong of me to override his rules and decisions of this kind: it might work disaster to important movements. And then, you ought to remember that I have other duties to attend to—heaven knows, enough for one man—and I can give no thought to questions of this kind. Why do you come here to appeal to my humanity?

"Don't you know we are in the midst of a war? That suffering and death press upon all of us? That works of humanity and affection, which we cheerfully perform in days of peace, are all trampled upon and outlawed by war? That there is no room left for them? There is but one duty now—to fight!

"Every family in the land is crushed with sorrow; but they must not each come to me for help. I have all the burdens I can carry. Go to the War Department. Your business belongs there. If they cannot help you, then bear your burden, as we all must, until this war is over. Everything must yield to the paramount duty of finishing this war."

Colonel Scott returned to his barrack, brooding.

When Matt finished reading the passage, he asked, "Is that a true story?"

Nana nodded.

"It just doesn't sound like the Abe Lincoln I read about in school," continued Matt. "I'm surprised by his behavior. I'm not talking about his decision to deny Scott leave. That may have been the right decision for a president to make during wartime. But it was the way he did it that seems offensive. I always pictured Lincoln as selfless, caring and compassionate, so I'm disturbed by the way Lincoln treated Scott."

"Your image of Lincoln is shaken a little."

"That's a generous way to put it," said Matt. "He showed absolutely no compassion about Scott's wife's sudden death. He seemed merciless."

Matt reread the section aloud:

> Am I to have no rest? Why do you follow me here with such business as this? . . . You ought to remember that I have other duties to attend to—heaven knows, enough for one man . . . I have all the burdens I can carry.

"What do you think was happening, Matt, that caused Lincoln to behave like that?" asked Nana.

"The burden of the war had to be weighing on him, with the daily reports of massive suffering and the rising death toll. At the end of the day, Lincoln had to be exhausted. So yes, I can see why he might have behaved as he did. He had some pretty good excuses for blowing up at Scott."

"There's a big difference between an explanation and an excuse. An explanation is the reason why something happened, and an excuse is an attempt to cover up and not be accountable. *A person can always find an excuse for bad behavior.*"

"You have a point," admitted Matt. "But that still doesn't sound like Lincoln."

"Do you think Lincoln would have liked this story to be a part of his obituary?"

"I seriously doubt it was the image he had of himself."

"Why don't you turn the page and read the next paragraph," suggested Nana. So Matt read the passage aloud:

Early the next morning, Colonel Scott heard a rap at the door. He opened it and there stood the President. He took Scott's hands, held them and broke out: "My dear Colonel, I was a brute last night. I have no excuse to offer.

"I was weary to the last extent, but I had no right to treat a man with rudeness who has offered his life to his country, much more a man in great affliction. I have had a regretful night and now come to beg your forgiveness."

He said he had arranged with Stanton for Scott to go to his wife's funeral. In his own carriage the Commander-In-Chief took the colonel to the steamer wharf of the Potomac and wished him Godspeed.

"What a great One Minute Apology!" said Matt. "It wasn't just his words. His *behavior* made the apology powerful."

"I thought you'd enjoy that," agreed Nana.

"Lincoln was willing to be honest and admit to himself that he'd done something wrong," said Matt. "He took full responsibility for his actions and sincerely recognized the need to apologize to the person he had offended."

"He also acted as soon as possible—*early the next morning,*" reviewed Nana. "He was specific: *'I was a brute last night. . . . I had no right to treat a man with rudeness who has offered his life to his country, much more a man in great affliction.'* And he showed how he felt about what he did: *'I have had a regretful night.'*"

"You memorized that passage," noted Matt.

"I told you I was a big Lincoln fan," said Nana. "In addition to being a great example of honesty in a One Minute Apology, Lincoln also demonstrated his integrity."

"How?"

"He didn't send for Scott, he went to Scott's quarters himself. The night before he kept insisting that Scott follow the chain of command, but in the light of the day, Lincoln couldn't have cared less about the hierarchy. In many ways, he was saying, 'The way I treated you last night was wrong—I am not proud of that man's behavior at all. The man you met last night isn't me at all.'"

"To admit any of those things would be tough," said Matt.

"That's true," Nana agreed. "When we're wrong, we're often too proud to admit it because what we did was the opposite of who we believe we are. And when we feel that way, we can't be honest with ourselves, much less anyone else."

"So if you take this further," reflected Matt, "if we can't admit we've done something wrong, we can't forgive ourselves. We get so down on ourselves that we end up feeling guilty, rather than admit we did something wrong. Then we can't forgive ourselves, when that's the only way to feel good again."

"You're right," said Nana. "The concept of forgiving yourself sounds simple but it's not always easy to do."

"What makes it so difficult?" asked Matt.

Nana answered, "We have to deal with two facts: First, we did something wrong that needs to be corrected. Second, we did something that is at odds with who we are or want to be, and how we'd like to be perceived."

"I imagine Lincoln had to wrestle with those two facts during what he called his regretful night," said Matt.

"Undoubtedly," said Nana. "He must have thought about who he really was and then chosen to become that person again. And then he took his early-morning visit to Scott's quarters."

"Do you think Lincoln changed his mind because of guilt?" Matt asked.

"No, I think it finally dawned on him how deeply Scott was grieving. He had to know how the pain of grief would impact Scott's effectiveness as a leader. Realizing how deeply he had hurt Scott, he decided to make amends personally."

"Come to think of it," said Matt, "Lincoln was earning back Scott's trust and was doing what was in the best interest of his army."

"Yes, making amends shows we're sincere about earning back lost trust," said Nana, "but we never get trust back until we change our behavior and make amends in a way the other person can appreciate."

Matt said, "Like the way Lincoln took Scott to the wharf in his own carriage?"

"Yes," said Nana. "Aren't you more likely to do business with a person who tries to recover your goodwill by making amends?"

"True. For example, recently an airline lost my reservation. I was very upset and said so to the ticket agent. She then surprised me by admitting that it was a systems error and apologizing for the inconvenience they had caused me. She said, 'This is so unlike us. I just put a note into the computer to make sure this doesn't happen again, but I want to know if we can do anything right now to regain your loyalty.'

"I was impressed and told her, 'You already have, because you listened to me, admitted the airline had erred, and asked how you could make up for it right now.'"

"She showed you immediately how sincere she was about earning back lost trust," said Nana. "Like you, most people appreciate a sincere apology and are eager to put the incident behind them and move on. The same thing goes for a One Minute Apology—it's incomplete without a sincere attempt to make things right—right away. As we say in our family:

❀

*Without A Change In*
*Your Behavior,*
*Just Saying*
*"I'm Sorry"*
*Is Not Enough*

❀

"Is that why people often dismiss it when someone just says 'I'm sorry'?" asked Matt.

"Yes," said Nana.

"If you're unreliable time and time again, and you say 'I'm sorry,' no one will take you seriously," Matt said.

"Right! Now let's go see how the others are doing."

Matt jotted down a few quick notes and followed the path past the garden to the boat to join Jack, Annie and Brad.

"Do you appreciate the value of integrity in a One Minute Apology?" Jack asked Matt.

"I sure do, thanks to Nana," said Matt. "Let me review my notes with you:

*The One Minute Apology*
*Ends With Integrity*

### You Have Integrity When You:

- *Recognize that the mistake you made is inconsistent with who you want to be.*

- *Reaffirm that you are better than your behavior and forgive yourself.*

- *Recognize how much you may have hurt someone, and make amends to that person for the harm you caused.*

- *Make the apology complete by changing your hurtful behavior.*

"Good work," said Jack.

Turning to Nana, Matt said, "Thank you for helping me understand integrity and for showing me the Lincoln story. I'll never forget it. I'm going to get a copy of it. There's someone I'd like to share it with."

"I'd be happy to make a copy for you. It's nice to know it means that much to you," said Nana. She looked at her watch and added, "You'd better head back. Carol wants these vegetables prepped for tonight's dinner."

Everyone gave Nana a good-bye hug and loaded the vegetables into the boat.

"See you later, Nana," Brad called out as they pulled away from the dock. "These veggies are great. I'm going to cook 'em on the grill."

"I'll grow them if you cook them! Thank you all," Nana said, waving good-bye.

"I'll bet she hasn't had a sleepless night in her life," Matt said over the sound of the motor.

"Nana? As my dad used to say, 'Mom always sleeps like a log.'"

# Not Attached To Outcome

After they rinsed the vegetables, Matt and Jack had a quick sandwich and headed off to play golf.

When they got to the golf course, Jack turned to Matt and said, "Since you haven't played golf in a while, why don't we play N.A.T.O. golf instead of competitive golf?"

"N.A.T.O. golf?"

"Yes. N.A.T.O. stands for **N**ot **A**ttached **T**o **O**utcome. When most people play golf, they focus on results and how they look to others. Their score becomes who they are. I'd like you to see how well you hit the ball when you're focusing on the game instead of the results."

"That sounds like fun," said Matt. "But knowing you, there are sure to be some valuable lessons, too."

"True," said Jack with a smile. "N.A.T.O. isn't just about golf. It also applies to the One Minute Apology."

"So N.A.T.O. it is!" said Matt with a smile as he and Jack approached the first tee.

By the time they finished playing golf and returned to the house, 4th of July decorations were on the counter and dinner was getting started.

Carol handed Matt a bag of corn to shuck and asked, "So who won?"

"We both did," replied Matt.

"You played N.A.T.O. golf."

"We sure did! It's amazing what you can do when you don't worry about your swing, the outcome or the opinion of others. I played better—it was the most fun I've had playing golf in a long time. The N.A.T.O. approach can be applied to just about anything."

"Yes, it can," said Carol with a knowing smile. "Jack has a very unique way of teaching this insight. Have you thought of other ways to apply it?"

"Yes. N.A.T.O.'s already helping me enjoy what I'm doing here, right now, instead of worrying about what might happen next week at work. It also applies to what Jack has been teaching me about apologizing:

✷

*Apologize*
*Not For The Outcome*
*But*
*Because You Know*
*You Were Wrong*
*And It's*
*The Right Thing*
*To Do*

✷

## Apology At Home and Work

Nana arrived and immediately admired the red, white and blue table setting. "If this doesn't say Independence Day, I don't know what will." She was carrying a large envelope and handed it to Matt, saying, "I had the story of Lincoln copied for you."

"Thank you, how thoughtful!" he said appreciatively. "You can't imagine what this means to me." He opened the envelope and turned to Jack. "I would love to share this with the president of my company, David Roberts. Do you mind if I use your scanner and e-mail it?"

"Go right ahead," said Jack.

Just as Matt pushed the Send button, the doorbell rang. Carol opened the front door and welcomed their new neighbors, Gayle and Don.

Passing appetizers, Matt told them about his unexpected visit that weekend, saying he came for Jack's advice about a problem at work, but had ended up learning about the One Minute Apology.

"It's powerful information that I know will change the course of my life," he said.

"That's a pretty strong statement. Apology is a fascinating subject," said Don. "I'd be willing to bet most people, including myself, don't know the first thing about how to apologize, so avoid it. I don't like feeling awkward. Yet I know when I don't have the guts to admit I'm wrong, a small incident can get totally out of control."

"That's what happened to me in high school biology class," said Brad. "I was joking around and let the hamsters out of their cage and they ran wild around the classroom. I realized the turmoil I'd caused and tried to say I was sorry to my teacher. I can still remember the look in her eyes—like, 'Trouble maker, I don't believe a word you are saying!'

"I felt stupid, mumbling 'I'm sorry,' which came off as a feeble gesture. It had little or no impact."

"Did you ever get through to her?" asked Don.

"Yes, finally."

"How?" asked Gayle.

Brad said, "I went to her after class and repeated how bad I felt about letting the hamsters loose. I asked her if there was any way I could make it up to her. She said 'No, I think you've done enough for one day.' But I wouldn't take no for an answer. I persuaded her to let me do something special for her to make up for the disruption I'd caused. Her car was always dirty, so I asked her if I could clean it for her. She was surprised, but let me. By cleaning her car not just once, but also for the next few weeks, I finally regained her confidence."

"How did you know she trusted you again?" asked Annie.

"By the way she talked to me in class. I could see it in her expression. She finally smiled at me."

"That's a great story, Brad," said Don. "Maybe you can give me some advice. I just found out that an old friend of mine is angry with me because he thinks I did something unethical to him. He's never mentioned one word about it to me. I just heard about this yesterday from a mutual friend. Now I understand why he cut off contact with me. Even though I don't feel I did anything wrong, should I apologize?"

"Not if you didn't do anything wrong," answered Brad. "In your case an apology wouldn't be right. Why don't you ask him why he cut you off?"

"Don't apologize just to make someone feel better," said Annie. "That's a lie."

Don said, "Maybe I ought to call him and say I heard he was upset with me. I value his friendship and would like to know if I did something wrong, and if I did, I'll gladly apologize and fix the damage."

"That's what I'd do, too," said Brad. "Even if you can't rebuild your friendship, at least you'd know you gave it your best shot."

Gayle said, "The One Minute Apology could be useful for problems at work. I'm the human resources director at my company. What advice should I give a manager who heads up our marketing department? One of her colleagues feels that Susan has wronged him, but Susan doesn't remember the incident."

Jack answered, "First *ask* Susan to *listen* to her colleague and be flexible enough to realize she might have *unintentionally* caused a problem with him. Second, she can assure her colleague that she wouldn't deliberately hurt anyone, and that it bothers her to know he was hurt by something she might have done."

"That's a good point," said Matt. "Just because you don't remember an incident doesn't mean you didn't cause someone harm."

Jack nodded. "We might dismiss an incident as trivial, be too busy or distracted to think about how our actions might affect someone else. Dismissing someone's words, opinions and ideas can slight a person and make them feel like they don't count with you."

"If you realize you inadvertently did something wrong, assure the person that you want to correct the situation as soon as possible," said Annie. "It may take a while to change a behavior that's become a pattern. You can change if the person is important to you."

"What if you don't particularly like the person you've harmed?" asked Gayle.

"You apologize because it's the right thing to do," said Brad.

"I could use some help overcoming negative feelings about someone who drains my energy," said Gayle.

"Mom, why don't you tell Gayle what happened on your river trip in British Columbia?" suggested Jack.

"It was the first week of June but freezing cold," said Nana. "There had been a lot of snow in Canada that winter, so the river was six feet higher than normal. There were twenty-five of us—two families with children, and the rest were couples. One man was facially scarred and disfigured. Behind his back the children called him 'Scarface.' They were frightened by his looks and by the gruff way he spoke. He and his wife weren't sociable, and stayed to themselves.

"Midway through the trip we had to travel by van on a narrow dirt road to the next leg of the river. Along the way, the provision truck broke down. I was in the van behind and we couldn't get around the truck. We were far from the nearest town and no one expected us for days. Cell phones were out of range. We were stuck in the middle of the woods.

"It got colder and began to snow. Everyone bundled together to keep warm—everyone except the scarred man and his wife. They went for a walk!

"The boatmen tried time and again to get the truck started. No luck. We were all getting concerned. The scarred man returned and gruffly asked what the hold-up was. The boatmen didn't know why the truck wouldn't start. The man with the scarred face tried the engine. Nothing happened.

"He opened the hood and began to tinker. Next, he started to take apart the engine. Everyone was on the edge of panic. The kids started yelling that Scarface was wrecking the engine. Not wanting to freeze to death, I went up to ask what the heck he was doing. He turned to me and growled, 'Get me tweezers, a piece of wire, or a bobby pin!' His tone was harsh but his eyes were bright and full of confidence. I found the things he was looking for and a half-hour later, he had the truck running again. Everyone—and I do mean everyone, especially the kids—started applauding and cheering. 'You saved our lives!' they yelled.

"The scar-faced man blushed and smiled for the first time. 'It wasn't much,' he said quietly. 'Anyone could have done it.' Of course we all knew otherwise. From that moment on, his new nickname was Hero.

"The kids began to follow him around, and every night they listened while he told stories. As it turned out, he was a fireman. His face and most of his body had been severely burned saving eight children trapped in a fire in New York City.

"We gathered around the campfire on our last night. I'll never forget how the brattiest kid on the trip stood up and said he could never forgive himself if he didn't apologize in front of everyone for the terrible way he had treated Hero. He said Hero didn't just save his life, he saved him from being mean or name-calling anyone ever again.

"Hero stood up, took the kid in his arms, looked him in the eyes and said, 'When I was your age, I was a whole lot worse! And I owe you an apology, too— I was anything but friendly when I joined the group. I judged you, too. I didn't have the confidence to let you know that the real me was different from what you saw. I apologize and I assure you I won't be making that mistake again.'

"By the final morning of the journey, no one wanted the trip to end," said Nana.

"I can see why everyone grew to respect Hero," said Matt. "He changed everyone's opinion of him by his behavior, getting involved and helping. Then when he apologized, everyone trusted what he was saying."

"When we sincerely apologize, forgive ourselves, make amends and demonstrate we've changed, we get something extra: peace of mind," said Nana.

The group fell into a thoughtful silence.

Minutes later, Carol and Annie directed everyone to the buffet dinner, where they all quietly helped themselves.

*Peace of mind—that's certainly something my president doesn't have,* thought Matt. *Come to think of it, neither do I.*

Gayle was the first to speak. "What if you remember something you didn't do and feel it's way too late to do anything about it?"

"Can you give us an example?" asked Carol.

"Yes," Gayle said. "About ten years ago, the husband of a friend I worked with died. I was on a trip and promised myself I'd send her flowers and a personal note. I never did either and all these years I've regretted it. If I saw this person today on the sidewalk, I'd be tempted to cross to the other side of the street to avoid her out of sheer embarrassment."

Carol answered, "Pick up the phone and call her. *Never assume you know what another person is thinking.* It may make her feel very special that you called her to apologize. It's never too late to let someone know how much you care."

"Good. That's just what I'll do," Gayle replied. "I'm thinking of more situations where I can apply the One Minute Apology, at work and at home."

"That's a relief!" said Don.

"Very funny, Mr. Jokester, but you're forgetting that you only apologize when you do something wrong," said Gayle. "Anyway, yesterday our sales manager came to my office for advice. He said he gave his boss a marketing concept that was actually his assistant's idea, without giving her the credit. He was concerned that the promotion he was getting was due to her idea. He felt bad and didn't know what to do."

"What did you tell him?" asked Carol.

"I told him to be honest. So he went to his boss and told him the truth. His boss said the marketing concept was good but he was being promoted for consistently delivering more than what was expected. Now there was an even better reason for promoting him—he was a man with integrity."

Gayle smiled and continued, "He was relieved, but said he still wants to clear up the matter with his assistant. The One Minute Apology is what he needs to know."

At the mention of returning to work, Matt felt a sudden wave of anxiety. He reminded himself, *don't be attached to outcome*, and returned his attention to the discussion at the table.

"In our plant," said Don, "many problems are a result of conflict, obnoxious behavior, and pettiness, while others are a result of accidents, mistakes, assumptions, forgetfulness or just plain stupidity."

"In those cases is there ever a reason not to apologize?" Matt asked.

Annie countered with a question of her own. "If you made a stupid mistake, would you want to repeat it?"

"No," answered Matt.

"Would you feel badly if your mistake caused harm to others?" asked Annie.

"Yes, of course."

"Okay," smiled Annie. "So what's the answer?"

*"Anytime I make a mistake, a One Minute Apology is required.* It seems to me," said Matt thoughtfully:

*The Best Way*
*To Apologize To*
*Someone You Have Harmed*
*Is To Tell That Person*
*"I Made A Mistake,*
*I Feel Bad About It*
*And I'm Committed To*
*Not Letting It*
*Happen Again"*

"That's a good way to remember the fourth secret," said Jack.

Matt added, "Here's what I'm getting: If I'm more sensitive about the effects of my behavior, maybe others will follow my example. And like a domino effect, each person becomes an example to those around him or her, and so on. Ultimately, we'll eliminate any need to apologize because we're all being thoughtful and considerate of one another, regardless of the circumstances. It's all about apology prevention, and that could rock our world!"

"You *got* it. You *really* got it!" exclaimed Jack, beaming at Matt.

"Okay, everyone, time to go out on the dock and watch the fireworks!" said Matt. "I'm celebrating the most liberating day I've had in a long time."

As the others rushed down to the dock, Matt took a memo pad from his shirt and wrote:

✿

*Every One Minute Apology*
*You Give Or Receive*
*Makes You More Aware*
*Of*
*How Your Behavior*
*Affects Other People*

✿

## *Taking Responsibility*

Sunday morning Matt woke up to the sound of thunder. It was dark, gray and windy, with lightning in the distance. He looked at the alarm clock. It was only 6:30 A.M., yet he felt rested. He leapt out of bed to enjoy his last day at the lake. He went into the kitchen and as he was making a pot of coffee, he heard a voice behind him.

"There's nothing like the smell of coffee in the morning!" It was Annie.

"What are you doing up so early?"

"I was about to ask you the same thing. Let's have our coffee on the covered porch and listen to the rain."

"Yes. The sound of the rain is very calming," said Matt, opening the door to the porch.

"Is the weekend what you had hoped for?" Annie asked.

"Funny you should ask. On my flight here I was thinking, 'This is great. I'll be seeing the One Minute Manager, my dad's best friend and the world's best management consultant, and with his advice all my problems will be solved.' As it turned out, I've learned something from each of you."

"My mother says that when the student is ready, the teachers appear."

"We've covered a lot this weekend. It's obvious that if you're not honest with yourself, you can't be honest with others. As difficult as it may be, the first thing I'll do when I make a mistake is come to grips with being wrong and correct the situation right away. Instead of making excuses or trying to justify inappropriate behavior, I'll have a sense of urgency about apologizing and make amends so the other person knows I'm sincere. No one I've offended will completely trust me again until I convince them I've changed. Regardless of what I say, I can only do so by changing my behavior."

"You've learned a lot," Annie said. "That's why I enjoy coming home whenever I can. We always seem to be talking about meaningful subjects. Last time I visited, for instance, we talked about culpability."

"What's that?" asked Matt.

"It's a fancy way of saying that each of us has a responsibility no matter where we are. When problems develop, we have to ask ourselves what we did to contribute to or exacerbate the problem. Sometimes it's because of an action we've taken, but more often than not, it's the result of something we didn't do. When we don't own up to how we contributed to the problem, we're not being honest."

"Sometimes it's difficult to tell the truth," said Matt. "No one enjoys being the one reporting bad news because most people don't accept bad news very well."

Matt paused as a startling thought occurred to him. "Annie, are you trying to tell me in a nice, polite way that I may have contributed in some way to my problem at work? Like, maybe I didn't do something I should have done. Are you saying that I'm culpable?"

"That's not for me to say. I really don't know what happened. You know Dad would never break a confidence," replied Annie.

"Still, what you say strikes a chord. I have to consider my own culpability. I won't run away from the idea. But blaming others is *soooo* much easier," he said.

Annie laughed. "Only in the short run. In the long run—well, I don't need to tell you the rest," she laughed.

"Thank you for the wake-up call," Matt replied.

"You're welcome. But it's nothing you wouldn't have figured out for yourself in time."

"Yes, but I have a deadline. I have to turn into a genius by tomorrow morning when I meet with my boss," he protested.

A flash of lightning and an ear-splitting crack of thunder interrupted their talk.

"It doesn't look like you and Dad are going to play much golf today."

"Knowing the way your father thinks, he'll say 'Great day for golf—with this weather we'll have the entire course to ourselves!'"

"That's true!" said Annie, laughing.

At that moment Jack joined them. "Well, it looks like we'll have the golf course to ourselves!" he boomed.

"What did I tell you?" said Matt.

"I take back what I said. Maybe you will become a genius by tomorrow!" quipped Annie.

"What's all this laughter about?" Carol called out from the kitchen. "Certainly not the weather. Come on in."

They made their way inside to pitch in with making French toast, a pleasure he hadn't experienced at home for a long time.

# Confidence

As everyone passed around the orange juice, syrup and freshly made French toast, Matt said how much he enjoyed last night's discussion at their dinner with the neighbors. "I have another question, though," he said. "What stops people from being honest, admitting they're wrong and apologizing?"

"It's an inside job," answered Jack.

"An inside job?"

"It has to do with how you feel about yourself inside—your self-worth," said Jack.

"Where does a person's self-worth come from?" asked Matt, pouring himself another cup of coffee.

"From four sources," replied Jack. "The first is fate. At birth, you don't have a choice of where you are born, who your parents are, whether you are male or female or the color of your skin. It's fate.

"The second is your early life experiences with adults—your parents, relatives, teachers and coaches.

"Third are your successes and failures in life.

"The fourth source of your self-worth is your perception of the first three."

"You've given this subject a lot of thought," said Matt.

"I have," said Jack. "Which of these four sources do you think is the most powerful in affecting your self-worth?"

"The fourth," Matt replied.

"Absolutely," said Jack. "It's from your perception of your fate, early life experiences and successes and failures that you make all of your choices."

"Choices?" asked Matt.

"Yes," replied Jack, "those three perceptions determine whether or not we appreciate ourselves and find ourselves worthy. We make the final choice—no one else."

"Why would anyone choose to be negative about him or herself?" asked Matt.

"That's where belief in your own personal value— apart from your past experiences—comes in," said Carol.

Brad said, "Our grandfather used to say that when a person loses perspective and sees himself as the center of the universe, that's the sign of an out-of-control ego."

"*People who have trouble apologizing think that who they are is a function of their performance plus the opinion of others,*" said Jack. "They are concerned about appearances and about keeping up with the Joneses."

Matt joked, "Somebody at work recently told me, 'I'm tired of trying to keep up with my neighbors because they keep buying things I can't afford.'"

They all laughed and Jack laughed the loudest.

Then he continued, "When people look to others for approval, their self-worth varies from day to day, depending on how others react to them. All they can think about is themselves. And yet:

✻

*People With Humility*
*Don't Think Less*
*Of Themselves.*
*They Just Think*
*About Themselves*
*Less*

✻

"How can you keep that kind of perspective?" asked Matt.

"*You separate who you are from what you do,*" answered Jack.

"You mean living N.A.T.O.—**N**ot **A**ttached **T**o **O**utcome?" asked Matt.

"Absolutely," said Jack with an appreciative smile. "When I ask parents, 'Do you love your kids?' they laugh because the answer is obvious—of course they do. Then I ask, 'Do you love your kids only when they get good grades or do well in athletics? In other words, if they are successful, you'll love them; if they aren't, you won't?' They laugh again and say, 'No. We love our kids no matter what.' That's unconditional love. What do you think would happen, Matt, if you accepted that kind of unconditional love for yourself?"

"I'd feel more secure and positive about myself," answered Matt, adding, "actually, I'd be *confident all the time!*"

"That's for sure," said Jack. "I believe we all come from unconditional love. Yet it's as if we're born with amnesia. We forget about that perfect love we came from. Eventually we all remember; it's just that for some of us it takes longer than others. Why wait?"

"I never thought of it that way," said Matt.

"When you think the love you get is conditional, then your self-worth is always up for grabs. That's when you start promoting or protecting yourself all the time. You believe you have to impress others to get love. And you think that to keep love, you have to give that good impression again and again. That's a sad way to live," said Jack.

"That sounds like a shaky emotional foundation," Matt said. "Not to mention how exhausted you must get."

Brad spoke up. "As our grandfather used to say, 'God didn't make junk.'"

"At some point," Carol said, "you wake up and finally understand there's no way you can achieve enough, gain enough recognition, obtain enough power, or own enough things to get any more love. You have all the love you need. And you had it from the minute you were born."

"What you just said may be the most important thing I have to learn," Matt said.

"And the most important thing your president has to learn, too," added Jack.

Matt glanced out the window. A streak of lightning flashed against the black clouds and the rain began to pour down.

## Apologizing To Yourself

After breakfast Jack and Matt left to pick up Nana so she could join the family for church. They didn't want her to drive in the rainstorm. Carol and Brad went with Annie in her car.

As they buckled their seat belts, Matt said, "Annie brought up another very interesting point this morning. She talked about culpability and helped me see how I could have contributed to the problem at work by not taking early action myself."

"My little Annie! She said something mean like that?" asked Jack, pretending to be incredulous. "Did you threaten to leave?"

"No. Your 'little Annie' put it so gently that I never once felt like I was in the hot seat—until, of course, I put myself there."

"Well, she certainly didn't learn that from me!" Jack joked.

"You're right about that. But thanks to Annie, I'm beginning to reconcile what happened at work. I played along, going along with the program, protecting the deceptions, concerned about losing my big salary and benefits. I convinced myself nothing was wrong.

"Of course, I suspected something was wrong," Matt continued. "I just didn't want to admit it to myself or anyone else. I, like everybody else, looked the other way. By not confronting the truth, I unconsciously helped my president get into trouble. As I told you Friday night, I was afraid to bring him any bad news. Maybe if I had spoken up, things would be different."

"You can't control the outcome of events," Jack said as he pulled the car into his mother's narrow driveway, "but *you can control what you think and what you do.*"

Jack continued, "You allowed your fear to drive your behavior. At the very least, you'd be feeling a lot better today if you'd been completely honest with yourself. Situations like the one at your company don't just happen in a week. It's very probable that many people knew, but, like you, no one wanted to rock the boat for fear of angering the boss and losing their job. What's the president of your company really like? Do you think he has it in him to pull it together?"

Matt answered, "Before all this happened, I had great respect and admiration for him. I owe him a lot, and I'll still be loyal to him. But to answer your question, I don't know anymore. Over the past year or so, he's become too preoccupied with the perks of his position. I wish I'd been more helpful to him. I guess I just didn't think I was in much of a position to do anything."

Jack said, "Don't be so hard on yourself. You know what to do now. Apologize to yourself for any behavior you're not proud of. Resolve to avoid repeating that behavior. Then repair the damage you've done to yourself and others by behaving differently. That's how you make things better. Now where does all of this leave you? Are you feeling better or worse than when you first arrived here?"

"I'm more confident about what I have to do. Learning about the One Minute Apology has made a huge difference in how I feel about myself. I feel more empowered than I have in years."

"And what's the only thing that's really changed over this weekend?" asked Jack.

"Me. I've changed how I think."

Jack challenged him, "How are you going to change your behavior?"

Matt thought about what he would do differently. After a few minutes, he said, "Let me get back to you on that."

# Asking For a One Minute Apology

As the car pulled into Nana's driveway, the rain was coming down hard. Matt leaped out of the car and ran to her cottage. As he stepped onto the front porch, the door opened and Nana appeared in a white plastic poncho. He opened his umbrella and walked her to the car, all the while thinking about Jack's question.

As they pulled out of Nana's driveway, Matt said, "You've both helped me to understand the power of apologizing. But what about the people who haven't received an apology when they deserve one? Last night I was thinking about how many people are hurt or heartbroken because the person who disappointed them didn't have the courage to apologize. What can they do?"

"May I answer?" asked Nana.

"By all means, please do," Jack replied.

"Those people could begin by asking for an apology," she responded.

"*Asking* for an apology?" wondered Matt.

"Yes," said Nana. "And after you ask, you tell the person what he or she did and how their actions hurt you."

Matt said, "Yes, Nana, but suppose you ask for an apology and the person won't give it to you? Or, even worse, they attack you for asking?"

"That's what everyone fears," said Nana, "but you have to speak up for yourself. Don't wait until you're as old as I am to say what's on your mind! Imagine if someone harmed you and then that person died. What good would it do to resent them? You're not hurting that person. That person is gone forever. The result of resentment is that in the end, you only hurt yourself."

"You're right," agreed Matt.

"When you have the courage to ask for an apology, you are also showing respect for yourself—whether you get the apology or not," added Jack. "You are also letting that person know how important your relationship is."

"That's true," said Matt. "No one would bother to ask for an apology from someone they didn't care about."

"*Asking for someone's apology is your chance to stand up for yourself and the relationship.* And there's another way to think about it: Suppose I offered you a bet that you would either win or break even. Would you take that bet?" asked Jack.

"Sure," said Matt. "I'd be a fool not to take it. There's no way to lose."

"Right," agreed Jack. "That's the identical situation you have when you're asking for an apology. If you get one you win; if you don't, you broke even."

Nana chimed in, "If you don't receive an apology and you think you deserve one, don't wait for the other person to think of it. Ask for it right away! Life is too short to wait for anyone to guess what you want, particularly someone you care about. As we discussed last night, many people have difficulty admitting they did something wrong. So, just tell them you want a One Minute Apology. And if they don't know how, let them know that admitting they made a mistake is the most important part. Once they get past that, the rest is easy. And you'll both feel better for it. Remind yourself that:

*

*Asking For An Apology*
*From Others*
*Shows Them How Important*
*They Are*
*To You*
*And Demonstrates*
*Your Own Sense*
*Of Self-Worth*

*

"What if you don't get the apology you think you deserve?" asked Matt.

"If the other person doesn't care enough about the relationship to apologize to you after they know they've hurt you, the relationship itself is in question. Maybe it's not the relationship you thought it was," said Jack.

"I see. If they refuse to apologize, that means they don't value me or our relationship," said Matt. "I hope I never have that experience."

"If it does occur, you'll take the information like an adult and move on," said Jack.

As they pulled up to the church, Nana said, "I can't wait to hear from our visiting minister today. The ladies at my book club were talking about him the other night. I think we're in for a real treat."

When they entered the church they joined Carol, Brad and Annie, who had saved seats for them. They were all wet from the storm but soon forgot their discomfort once the minister began speaking.

# A Chance To Finally Get It Right

Nana was right about the minister. Matt enjoyed the sermon and was especially moved by his closing story:

"When I was a young boy, I had a fabulous grandmother," said the minister. "She was an incredible Monopoly player. Whenever the two of us played, she completely wiped me out. By the end of the game, she owned everything—Broadway, Park Place, you name it! She would always smile at me and say, 'John, someday you're going to learn how to play the game.'

"One summer, a new kid moved next door to me. It turned out that he was an incredible Monopoly player. We began to play every day and I really improved! I was thrilled because I knew my grandmother was coming for a visit in September.

"When my grandmother arrived, I ran into the house, gave her a big hug and said, 'Do you want to play Monopoly?' I'll never forget how her eyes lit up. I set up the board and we began to play. But this time, I was ready for her.

"By the end of the game, I had wiped her out! I owned *everything*. It was the greatest moment of my life!

"At the end of the game my grandmother smiled and said, 'John, now that you know how to play the game, let me teach you a lesson about life—it all goes back in the box.'

"'What?' I asked. I'll never forget her reply:

"'Everything you bought, everything you accumulated—at the end of the game, it all goes back in the box.'"

The minister looked over the congregation. "Isn't that the way it is with life?" he asked. "No matter how much you push and shove for money, recognition, power, prestige and possessions, when life is over, everything goes back in the box. The only thing you get to keep is your soul. That's where you store who you loved and who loved you.'"

On the ride back from the church through the driving rain, Matt was quiet. The only sound was the swishing of the windshield wipers.

In almost a whisper, Matt said, "That story the minister told at the end crystallizes everything we've talked about this weekend, doesn't it?"

"Yes, it does," Jack replied. "I'm glad you noticed. Since everything we accumulate in our lives—from our performance and the opinion of others—goes back in the box, we might as well do what is right. The sooner we recognize that it's our ego that gets us off course, the sooner we realize the only way to repair the damage we have done to ourselves and others is to be honest, admit we were wrong, apologize and commit to change our behavior."

*"The beauty of the One Minute Apology is it's the best way I know to make things better for you and the people you care about,"* said Jack.

They rode the rest of the way home in thoughtful silence.

## The Best Way To Say Thank You

The storm was much worse by the time they got home. As they hurried inside Matt's cell phone rang. It was David Roberts, the president, calling.

Matt looked apprehensively toward Jack and left to take the call in the guestroom. He returned in a few minutes, looking confused.

Jack asked, "Is everything all right?"

"Yes. At least I think so. Mr. Roberts said he heard about the bad storm on the weather report. He didn't want me to take any unnecessary traveling risks. He also told me he'd understand if I couldn't make the meeting tomorrow morning. And then, Nana," Matt said with a big grin, "he said how he appreciated the Lincoln story. He said he read it several times, shared it with his family and plans to reread it tonight."

"That's already a good indication that he's in a better frame of mind," said Jack.

"I hope you're right. Roberts's words were considerate and grateful but he sounded tired."

"Or emotionally exhausted," added Carol.

"That's entirely possible," said Matt. "If I'd stayed in the city, I'd probably sound like that—or worse. I've always heard it was important to have time away, but until this weekend I've never been so convinced of the benefits of getting away for a fresh perspective."

Meanwhile Carol took another look outside and suggested getting more weather information. Brad volunteered to check the computer for the latest forecast and found that the storm would continue for two more days. When Matt heard that, he called the airport.

"All flights are canceled. Is there a train station anywhere in the vicinity?" Matt asked.

"There is," said Jack.

"I need to get going. If there's any chance of making that meeting tomorrow, I have to catch the next train."

Matt called and reserved a seat on the last train for the city and called for a taxi. Then went to his room and quickly packed.

When Matt rejoined the family in the living room, Annie kidded, "I think he's leaving because he knows Dad will still brave this weather for a round of golf."

"Want to take a rain check?" Brad asked Matt. Everyone laughed as the rain poured down on the roof.

"I'd gladly take you up on that and come back— and yes, even play golf in the rain, if necessary," Matt replied, laughing. When the taxi honked, he grabbed his bags, turned to Jack and said, "Wish me luck!"

"What you have now is much better than luck. You have knowledge," replied Jack. "You now know about the fourth secret—the One Minute Apology."

"I now know what to do," responded Matt.

"You already knew what to do, deep down. You only needed to be reminded," said Jack.

"Well, thank you so much for *reminding* me," said Matt.

Jack nodded his acknowledgment and said, "The best way you can thank me is to use the One Minute Apology and share it with others."

"I will," promised Matt.

The taxi honked its horn again. Matt hugged each of them, said his good-byes, picked up his bags again and ran through the deluge to the waiting taxi.

On the way to the train station, he felt gratitude for all he had learned. On the train, however, he began to feel anxious again. Then he reminded himself about what he had learned and again felt calm and confident.

Using his notes from the weekend, he began to write a summary of what he had learned.

He thought, *David J. Roberts, president and CEO, may not want to hear what I have to say, but I am no longer attached to the outcome and it's the right thing to do.*

Matt was confident that he now accepted himself unconditionally, regardless of what anyone else thought. He took out his notebook and reread his personal notes on self-worth:

# Self-Worth

- *My self-worth is not based on my performance or the opinion of others.*

- *When I make a mistake, I am willing to admit it, regardless of the outcome.*

- *I don't think less of myself, I think of myself less.*

- *I realize it's impossible to achieve enough, gain enough recognition, attain enough power or own enough things to earn any more love.*

- *I am already loved unconditionally.*

# The Moment Of Truth

**M**onday morning, Matt arrived at the office promptly at 7:00 A.M. He'd been up late completing a summary of what he had learned for the president. Making his way down the long, empty corridor to the president's suite he thought to himself: *It's so quiet, no one would ever guess that everything could break loose tomorrow. Here goes!*

Matt stood in the doorway of the president's office. Papers, reports and charts were scattered on his desk and the conference table. It looked like David Roberts had been working there all night—maybe the entire weekend.

As Matt entered the room, the president looked up in surprise. Then his face broke into a big, welcoming smile—something Matt hadn't seen for a long time.

Matt quietly shut the door and sat down.

"I'm glad you arrived home safely and that you're here now," said Roberts, looking directly into Matt's eyes. "At first, I wasn't sure you would return, and if you didn't, I would understand. And thank you again for sending me the Lincoln story."

"I'm glad you found it meaningful."

"It was more helpful than you might imagine. When it arrived, I was writing my letter of resignation," said the president. "But after I read what Lincoln did, it woke me up and I reconsidered my options. I still face a big dilemma. But there are viable alternatives. Not so much for myself, but for all the people who have trusted me all these years."

"I hoped you'd have a change of heart," said Matt. "That's why I wanted to come here this morning. I've had an extraordinary experience these past couple of days and I've come away with some very powerful ideas that may be of use."

"Once I read the Lincoln story, I knew that you were doing some serious thinking yourself," said Roberts.

"Yes, and I hope you'll agree to hear me out," said Matt. "I have to warn you right now, though, that some of what I'm about to suggest may not be pleasant for you to hear."

"Nothing you can say can possibly be harder to hear than the things I've been telling myself these past few days. However, I appreciate your forthrightness. Shoot!"

Matt began, "One of the first things I learned this weekend is that I owe you an apology. You say you admire my forthrightness, but I haven't been that way lately, with myself or with you. I've been part of the problem, not the solution. I saw things that were wrong but didn't have the guts to tell you the truth or confront you with reality.

"Although you're the president of our company, you're not in this alone. I felt that what was going on around here wasn't right and feel ashamed that I didn't tell you the truth earlier, but I was afraid of losing your trust or my job. Possibly both. I apologize for failing you. I can assure you it won't happen again."

The president looked stunned for a few moments, blinked hard twice and said simply, "Thank you."

Choked up from the president's reaction, Matt gathered his composure. "I would like to make a suggestion, and I hope you can take it in the manner it's intended," he said.

The president swallowed hard and looked up at Matt. "What is it?" he asked.

"You need to apologize to the board."

The president shut his eyes for a second, then said, "I know you're right, but I wouldn't begin to know how to do what Lincoln did. I finally realized last night that I've spent a lifetime skillfully avoiding apologizing to anyone about anything. I guess you could say it's finally caught up with me."

Matt smiled confidently and said, "You're talking to the right person. That's exactly what I learned this weekend. Let me summarize for you what constitutes an effective apology."

Roberts listened intently to Matt for over an hour. When Matt finished, the president let out a big sigh.

"What you have brought me today is the missing link between my head and my heart, and I can't express my appreciation adequately. While you have been learning about the One Minute Apology, I've been working on something, too—something I know I'm good at—maybe the only thing I'm good at. I have a business plan that I believe will turn this entire crisis around and get our company back on track and make it stronger than ever.

"But my plan is useless unless I can rebuild the board's trust in me. My behavior was so arrogant, egotistical and completely inappropriate last Friday. I seriously doubt the board of directors will listen to anything I have to say."

Matt was silent for a few moments and then responded, "They will begin to listen if you apologize sincerely. That may be difficult, considering the time and what's at stake, but:

❖

*The One Minute Apology
Is An Effective Way
To Correct A Mistake
And Restore The Trust Needed
For A Better Relationship*

❖

The president looked at his young colleague and said, "I realize now how wrong I've been and how much harm I've caused. Please stay and coach me through this One Minute Apology."

"I'd be honored," replied Matt.

During their discussion, the president asked many insightful questions. The more they talked, the more Matt realized that the president genuinely wanted to learn how to apologize effectively. It was evident that Roberts was not regarding this as an expedient way out of his difficult problem. Matt breathed a sigh of relief. He knew that if the president was insincere, it would only make matters worse.

When they finished, the president turned to Matt and said, "Between now and tomorrow, I will be thinking about my One Minute Apology to the board. I will give what you said every consideration. Meanwhile, would you stay to meet with our team while we plan the events that need to occur over the next few days and possibly the months to come? The others will be joining us shortly."

"I'd enjoy that," replied Matt.

When the department heads arrived, the president began the meeting by saying briefly to the team members, "You're all here with me on your holiday to help with a meeting that wouldn't be necessary if I hadn't made some serious mistakes. Thank you for coming."

Then the president surprised Matt by apologizing to his whole team. He had not expected Roberts to apologize until he was in front of the board. It was awkward, but the president sincerely did his best to let everyone know he was wrong and wanted to change his behavior.

The team members looked startled at first. Then cautiously, one of the department heads said, "We came here to do a job, so let's move ahead."

The other team members agreed. After the president's brief but honest opening, they all—for the first time—spoke their minds freely. At times the discussion about the restructuring became heated, and the meeting went well into the night. But in the end the team had a plan they were all proud to be part of.

# The President's One Minute Apology

On Tuesday morning Matt returned to the president's office prior to the board meeting. David Roberts got up and met Matt halfway, and said, "I owe *you* a special apology."

Matt was taken aback as the president continued, "I know you gave up a number of other interesting opportunities at other companies to come and work for me. I let you down recently in many ways, and regardless, you stayed loyal to me. You are an extraordinary young man. No matter what happens today, I will make sure everyone knows what you did for me and ultimately tried to do for the company. I promise I won't let you or others down again. I hope I can demonstrate that further in the board meeting in just a few minutes."

"Thank you," Matt replied. "I hope it goes well."

"I appreciate that."

Then Matt and the president entered the boardroom.

After the chairman brought the meeting to order, the president rose to address the board members. Matt sensed the hostility in the room as the president walked to the head of the table.

Roberts swallowed hard and began, "By now you are all aware of the gravity of the current situation our company faces. I take full responsibility for my mistakes in judgment that have contributed to the severity of the problem.

"I am ashamed of my actions. You all experienced an example of my outrageous behavior last Friday, and for that I am regretful and embarrassed. Frankly, my inflated ego has been my downfall of late. I didn't listen, and even worse, I didn't invite the kind of information that could have prevented our substantial loss last quarter and the problems that lie ahead."

The president had the complete attention of the board members as the full impact of what he was saying began to sink in.

Roberts continued, "I recognize how much I have hurt this company and harmed you, my colleagues, associates—and potentially our customers, suppliers and stockholders—and for that, I apologize. I know there are many things that require immediate change, and that begins with me.

"You are about to receive a comprehensive restructuring plan, which I am confident will not only quickly restore the company to its former preeminent position, but will ultimately put us in a league of our own. This plan can be implemented by whoever is CEO. I am prepared to submit my resignation today. In fact, I have already signed a letter to the board to that effect.

"Before I present the proposed plan to you, please know that if you care to keep me in a leadership role, you and my colleagues have my solemn promise that I will never repeat the poor management actions I have taken over these past months."

As the president concluded his One Minute Apology, the expressions on the board members' faces relaxed. The air of hostility that had pervaded the room earlier began to change.

The president asked Matt to distribute a folder containing a copy of his restructuring plan to each board member. As they were being distributed, the president began to describe in detail the new proposal and the plans for its implementation.

When he finished speaking, the room became quiet. The chairman took the floor and requested that Roberts and Matt leave the room while he and the members of the board met in private.

The president and Matt paced the corridor. Matt spoke first. "You did the right thing, regardless of the outcome."

Roberts answered, "I appreciate that and I hope I get the chance to let my actions speak louder than my words."

Thirty minutes later, they were called back and the chairman again took charge of the meeting. "I speak on behalf of everyone here today. We're impressed by what you've just said. We appreciate your apology and accept it. If you follow through on what you suggest, we will be one hundred percent behind the innovative and impressive restructuring plan you've given us this morning."

The chairman then asked the president, "Do you have anything further to say?"

"Yes, I do," responded Roberts. He paused for a few moments, looking toward each of the board members individually, and then said, "I intend to work without pay until this current situation is turned around."

The board members looked astounded.

"Furthermore," Roberts continued, "by contract I am protected by generous bonus and severance clauses. But today I relinquish my rights to those rewards. Those benefits and privileges were based on trust in the person you hired—the person I once was and intend to be again.

"That person warranted and deserved your complete trust and respect. But that person went off the track somewhere along the way. I intend to become that man again—but no one in this room should have to subsidize his return. I must do it myself. You can judge when I am that person again and restore my compensation at the appropriate time."

The room was silent. Then, spontaneously, everyone rose to their feet and applauded.

The president, unfazed, looked to Matt and all the eyes in the room followed his. He said, "I'd like to thank my special assistant, Matt Hawkins, who went to great lengths to help me through this perilous situation."

Matt stopped taking notes. Recalling the special weekend at the lake with an extraordinary family, he looked upward thinking, *Thank you, Dad, for sending me your good friend, Jack.*

At that moment Matt completely understood the full impact of Jack's parting words to him right before he left the lake:

*The Best Way To Thank Me*
*Is To Use The One Minute Apology*
*Whenever You Need To*
*And Share What You've Learned*
*With Others*

# Epilogue

That evening Matt sent an e-mail to Jack thanking him and his family for all the help they had given him over the weekend. He went on to say that Jack would understand the impact of his advice when he read about the success of his company in the months to come.

He ended his e-mail saying, "I have included a copy of my notes from the weekend. I thought you might find them useful. My president and I certainly did. You're the best. God bless."

My apology begins by answering
truthfully the following questions:

What was the real mistake I made?

What part did I play in creating the problem?

Did I think it through?

Why did I do it?

Was this act a result of my fears?

What was I thinking?

How long have I let this go on?
Is this the first time?
Or is this behavior becoming a habit?

Have I lost the trust of others?

Were other people affected by what I did?

What is the truth about myself I am not
dealing with?

How will I change my behavior to demonstrate
my commitment not to repeat my mistakes?

**Then I start with honesty:**

- *I am truthful and admit to myself I've done something wrong.*

- *I take responsibility for my actions.*

- *I apologize as soon as possible— regardless of the outcome.*

- *I tell the person(s) I harmed specifically what I did wrong.*

- *I say how I feel about what I did.*

**And I end with integrity:**

- *I know what I did is inconsistent with the kind of person I want to be.*

- *I am better than my behavior.*

- *I forgive myself.*

- *I make amends for all harm done.*

- *I demonstrate I have changed by changing my behavior.*

# Acknowledgments

We wish to give a praising to many of the people who helped us make this a better book, including:

Margie Blanchard and Nevins McBride, our spouses, who skillfully and lovingly make our lives apology free;

Debbie Blanchard Medina and Scott Blanchard; Kimberly McBride, Kelly Wright, Leslie McBride Ege and Robyn McBride Deuber, our children, with whom we have exchanged many meaningful apologies over the years and from whom have been given continued practice with our grandchildren Kurtis and Kyle Blanchard, Alec Medina, Phoebe, Annabel and Lucy Wright, Charlotte and Alexandra Ege and Wylie and Sylvie Deuber;

Donna DeGutis, Faye Atchison and Anne Bomke of the McBride Literary Agency for their publishing professionalism;

James Dobson for suggesting N.A.T.O. (**N**ot **A**ttached **T**o **O**utcome) as a wonderful way to play golf and live life; Dottie Hamilt for always being there for Ken in the past, and Margery Allen who now fills her shoes; Phil Hodges for his encouragement, guidance and continual help; Jennifer James for what she taught us about the sources of self-esteem; Spencer Johnson not only for his wonderful foreword but also for his wise counsel; Larry Hughes and Pat Golbitz for their initial editorial guidance; Martha Lawrence for her editorial help with this revised edition; Robert McGee for what we learned about self-worth; John Ortberg for sharing his story of playing *Monopoly* with his grandmother; the late Charlie and Vera Richardson for believing our book would change lives; the late Carl Sandburg for his wonderful story of Lincoln's apology;

Jane Friedman, president and CEO of HarperCollins, whose enthusiasm about our book has meant so much to us; our publisher, Michael Morrison, for his leadership; our editor, Henry Ferris, for his continued support of this book; and Peter Hubbard, for his editorial assistance.

# Services Available

If this book inspired you to apologize or ask someone for an apology, we'd love to hear your story. What happened and how did it go? Did it make your life and the lives of anyone else better? Tell us about it at oma@OneMinuteApology.com or write to us at the addresses below.

Ken Blanchard and Margret McBride speak at conventions and organizations around the world. For additional information on their speaking activities please contact:

The Ken Blanchard Speakers Bureau
The Ken Blanchard Companies
125 State Street
Escondido, CA 92029
1-800-728-6000 or
760-489-5005

Margret McBride
McBride Literary Agency
7744 Fay Avenue
Suite 200
La Jolla, CA 92037
858-454-1550

The Ken Blanchard Companies is a global leader in workplace learning, productivity, performance and leadership effectiveness. The mission of the company is to unleash the potential and power in people and organizations for the greater good. Based on the belief that people are the key to accomplishing strategic objectives and driving business results, Blanchard® programs develop excellence in leadership, teams, customer loyalty, change management and performance improvement. To learn more, visit www.kenblanchard.com.

"I am a volunteer at the Orange County Correctional Facility in Orlando, Florida; teaching a class weekly. I have taught many books over the years but never one as powerful as *The 4th Secret of the One Minute Manager*. This book sparked an emotion in several of the inmates that they had never felt before—something so special that it led them to apologize to their families and in some cases even to their victims' families."

—Warren N. Kenner, motivational speaker

*"The Fourth Secret* provides insights that make behavior change come naturally. It presents a concept that makes you say, "Why didn't I think of that?" This powerful little book can change not just how you act in business, but your personal relationships as well."

—James Kilts & John Manfredi, coauthors of *Doing What Matters: How to Get Results That Make a Difference*

"Until it becomes required reading in our schools, I recommend all families read it together."

—Lyn Tisdale Krant, COO, SK Sanctuary

"I recommend it to friends, family and clients. But it all began with how it added to my own life first. I'm sure every reader will find that added value."

—Peter Lambrou, Ph.D., vice chair of psychology, Scripps Memorial Hospital, La Jolla, California, and coauthor *of Instant Emotional Healing*